SURVIVAL HANDBOOK

JUNGLE

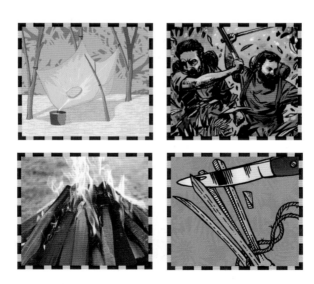

SURVIVAL
HANDBOOK
JUNGLE

Jen Green
Consultant: Andrew Price

Miles
KeLLy

First published in 2012 by Miles Kelly Publishing Ltd
Harding's Barn, Bardfield End Green,
Thaxted, Essex, CM6 3PX, UK

This edition published 2014

2 4 6 8 10 9 7 5 3 1

Publishing Director Belinda Gallagher
Creative Director Jo Cowan
Editorial Director Rosie Neave
Design Manager Simon Lee
Image Manager Liberty Newton
Production Manager Elizabeth Collins
Reprographics Stephan Davis,
Jennifer Hunt, Thom Allaway

ISBN 978-1-78209-434-0

Printed in China

British Library Cataloguing-in-Publication Data
A catalogue record for this book is available from the British Library

Important notice
This book provides useful information for hypothetical
situations in which individuals may find themselves. Some
of the techniques described in this book should only be
used in dire emergencies, when the survival of individuals
depends upon them. The publisher and author cannot be
held responsible for any injuries, damage, loss, or
prosecutions resulting from the use or misuse of any
of the information in this book.

Made with paper from a sustainable forest

www.mileskelly.net
info@mileskelly.net

CONTENTS

GET INFORMED

GET READY

GET SAFE

GET SETTLED

GET MOVING

GET OUT

IMAGINE YOU ARE STRANDED IN THE THICKEST OF JUNGLES.

How would you cope?

This book explores what it would be like to be in a survival situation, and tells you what to expect. Look out for the 'Try this at home' panels for tips and activities that you can practise safely in the comfort of your own home.

WARNING!

Never put yourself in danger and always ask the permission of a responsible adult before trying any of the activities in this book.

GET INFORMED

Environment

Jungle challenge

JUNGLES ARE ONE OF THE TOUGHEST ENVIRONMENTS on Earth. Hot, steamy conditions bathe you in sweat from dawn to dusk. Insects bite every inch of exposed skin. You have to fight your way through dense foliage, where dangerous creatures lurk in every shadow. Each moment could be a survival challenge. **Are you up to the test?**

◄ If food is scarce you may need to eat jungle foods. This expedition has caught a rat.

Why visit the jungle?

Europeans first entered jungles in search of gold, or for the thrill of mapping new territory. Modern survival experts go to test their skills. Some people get stranded in the jungle by accident. Whether on a planned expedition or in an emergency, learning the key survival skills in this book will help you stay safe and healthy, so you can make the most of your trip.

↓ A local guide keeps visitors safe deep in the African jungle.

Get a guide

To outsiders, the jungle is a scary, hostile world. Yet people have lived and thrived in jungles worldwide for centuries. To them, the forest is a haven that meets their needs for food, shelter and clothing. Survival experts say the best way to get to know the jungle is through a local guide.

Leafy wilderness

TRUE JUNGLES ARE found in the tropics. Also known as tropical rainforests, these dense, tangled forests grow in regions with abundant rainfall. The intense heat and moisture create ideal growing conditions, with trees shooting to 70 m or more.

Where in the world?

Jungles flourish in hot, wet regions around the Equator. In the last 150 years, huge areas of forest have been felled for timber, but vast, uncharted areas still remain. The jungles of Central and South America, Africa, Southeast Asia and Australia are some of the last truly wild places on Earth.

WOW!

Rainforests are a naturalist's heaven. In 1832, English scientist Charles Darwin wrote of visiting the Amazon: "Delight ... is a weak term to express the feelings of a naturalist who, for the first time, has wandered by himself in a Brazilian forest."

⬇ This map shows the world's largest areas of tropical jungle.

KEY

1 Central America
2 Amazon
3 Congo Basin
4 Madagascar
5 Southeast Asia
6 Australia

TYPES OF JUNGLE

Ancient untouched jungles are called primary forests. Secondary forests have been cut and grown back again. Upland jungles are called cloud forests.

Primary rainforest

Mighty trees cast deep shade in these untouched forests. Vegetation may be sparse on the ground, but trailing vines and roots still make the going tough.

Secondary rainforest

Plant growth is prolific in secondary forest along river banks and in sunny clearings. Progress on foot is slow because you need to hack your way with a machete.

Cloud forest

Mountains in the tropics are swathed in mist, which makes it impossible to see your way. Cold nights and wet clothing can cause chills. Food is scarce.

WETLAND FORESTS

High rainfall causes waterlogged conditions in inland jungles. Coastal forests are flooded daily by the tides.

Freshwater swamp

Inland bogs and marshes harbour mosquitoes and leeches. Avoid swamps by watching for tufts of reeds or tall grass.

Coastal forest

Mangrove forests grow on coasts in the tropics. Tangled roots above and below the water form an obstacle course. Food is plentiful, but so are predators such as crocodiles and snakes.

FREE YOURSELF FROM A SWAMP

1. If you stumble into a swamp and start to sink, try to stay calm. Struggling will only make you sink deeper.
2. Take time to spot the nearest firm ground, such as a bank or island with shrubs.
3. Spread your body weight over a wide area. Lay a shirt in front of you. Then slowly flop onto your front.
4. Use a slow breast-stroke action to free yourself and move forward. Make for dry ground and haul yourself out.

The mighty Amazon

THE AMAZON RAINFOREST covers nearly half of South America. It contains a fifth of all known plants and birds, and a tenth of all animals. One mistake in this vast leafy wilderness could cost you your life.

Amazon River

The world's mightiest river threads its way through the forest. Rising in the Andes Mountains, it flows 6500 km east to the Atlantic. On the way it is joined by more than 1000 tributaries. About 2000 species of fish inhabit these waters, including the dreaded razor-sharp toothed piranha.

⬇ Piranhas are deadly predators. A shoal can strip an animal to the bone within minutes.

⬆ The Amazon carries more water than any other river in the world.

Hidden horrors

People visit the Amazon to view spectacular wildlife such as parrots and butterflies. But the forest also harbours deadly snakes called constrictors. The emerald tree boa grows to 1.8 m in length. It wraps its muscular body around its prey, squeezes it to death – then swallows it whole.

⬆ The emerald tree boa's skin provides superb camouflage as it slithers through the branches.

↓ A local Achuar hunter demonstrates how to use a blowgun to capture prey in the jungle canopy.

Amazon hunters

The Amazon is home to hundreds of tribal groups. Many live by hunting game such as birds and monkeys high in the forest canopy. Moving silently through the forest, groups such as the Achuar track game by looking for signs the animals leave behind, such as dung and discarded fruits and nuts.

TIP

Rainy season in the Amazon lasts from October to May. The best time to visit is from June to September, when water levels are lower.

TRACKING FOREST ANIMALS

Practise moving quietly through the forest, tracking animals. Wear dull-coloured clothing and move slowly. Try to avoid treading on dry leaves and twigs that will rustle or crack, giving you away. Track animals by looking for signs such as fur, dung, or half-eaten nuts and berries.

➡ In the Amazon's rainy season, jaguar prints such as these are easy to identify.

Extreme weather

JUNGLE TEMPERATURES RANGE from 30°C by day to 20°C at night. The hot, sticky conditions make life uncomfortable. Torrential rain and thunderstorms are dangerous and can trigger worse hazards — **terrifying landslides and flash floods.**

Rainfall and humidity

Rainforests receive at least 200 cm of rain a year. In many forests it rains almost every day. Trees recycle moisture, absorbing it with their roots and releasing it through their leaves, so the air is usually saturated, with 100 percent humidity. Clothing is always damp, so lighting a fire is a priority to dry clothes.

↓ Trekking in torrential rain can be dangerous because of slippery conditions.

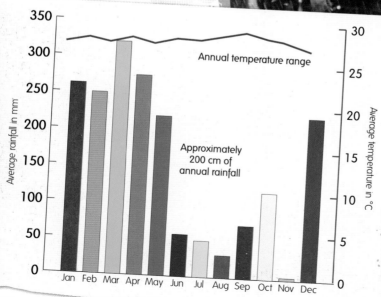

Annual temperature range

Approximately 200 cm of annual rainfall

Average rainfall in mm

Average temperature in °C

Jan Feb Mar Apr May Jun Jul Aug Sep Oct Nov Dec

← This graph shows the rainfall each month in a typical rainforest. The temperature stays fairly even throughout the year.

TIP
Never use an umbrella in a thunderstorm, as it could attract a lightning strike.

Thunderstorms

Thunderstorms are a frequent hazard. In the tropics these storms move very quickly, so prepare for a downpour at the first rumble of thunder.

⬆ Lightning streaks across the sky above the Brazilian jungle.

TRY THIS AT HOME — MEASURE A STORM

Estimate the distance of a storm by counting the seconds between the lightning flash and the thunderclap. Sound takes three seconds to travel one kilometre. Take cover if the storm is close.

Flash floods and landslides

Heavy rain fills rivers and streams, sometimes causing a flash flood. A quiet stream can quickly become a raging torrent that washes away roads and bridges. Trees can be swept along like battering rams. Leave the riverbank and head uphill. However, be aware that heavy rain can loosen rocks and soil on steep slopes. This can trigger a landslide or mudslide. Avoid climbing very steep slopes.

⬆ Ultra-heavy rainfall has caused this river in South America to burst its banks.

Beasts and bugs

JUNGLES ARE HOME TO half of all living things on land. Unfortunately, that includes many dangerous creatures, from ferocious mammals to creepy-crawlies. The good news is that almost all are wary of humans, and will slink away if given the chance.

BIG BRUTES

Always steer well clear of large animals. Although most will give you a wide berth, others may be curious as to why you're in their habitat.

Gorilla

These giant primates of Central Africa grow to 1.8 m in height. Powerful males will defend their group by charging at intruders.

Tiger

Top predators of Asian rainforests, tigers take prey as large as deer and cattle. The striped coat provides perfect camouflage. They are feared as man-eaters.

Elephant

These huge mammals are a menace in Asian rainforests. If startled, an elephant could charge and trample you underfoot.

Jaguar

The largest cat of Central and South American jungles grows to 1.8 m in length. These stealthy hunters are expert climbers and swimmers. Take extra care by riverbanks.

HOW TO AVOID DANGEROUS ANIMALS

1 Keep calm and back away slowly. Animals can sense your fear. Don't run or turn your back.

2 Never come between a mother and young.

3 Never tease or try to catch wild animals.

4 Making a lot of noise will deter most animals from attacking you.

⬇ Although this leech will drop off once it has had its fill of blood, the wound may continue to bleed. It's important to clean the bite area thoroughly.

Ticks and leeches

Ticks are round, eight-legged mites. Leeches are long, thin worms that live in damp places. Both are blood-sucking parasites that are attracted by body heat. If you pick them off, the jaws can remain in your skin and cause infection. Use a dab of salt or a lighted match to remove them. When they have drunk their fill, they drop off naturally.

WOW!

Vampire bats are a danger in tropical America as they are known to transmit rabies. These night-active creatures may sneak up on sleeping humans, pierce the skin and lap the blood. As with other biting creatures, the best defence is to keep well covered.

⬇ Malaria is caused by parasites passed on by the female anopheles mosquito.

Deadliest of all

The world's deadliest animal is not a large, ferocious beast, but the anopheles mosquito. Every year, 1–3 million people die after contracting malaria from mosquito bites. Scratching itchy bites can also lead to infection. The best defence is to use jungle-strength repellent and cover up. See page 37 for advice on improvised protection.

Beware poison

MANY CREEPING OR SLITHERING creatures are armed with deadly poison. Even plants contain deadly toxins to stop animals feeding on them. In this dangerous world, it pays to keep alert. **Be careful where you walk and what you touch.**

The golden poison arrow frog's skin is highly toxic, which protects it from predators.

PLANT DOS AND DON'TS

Many jungle plants have stinging hairs, tiny barbs or poisonous sap. In general, avoid:

1 Plants that contain milky sap.
2 Plants with thorns, hairs or spines.
3 Beans or seeds inside a pod.
4 Plants with red leaves, or those that give off a smell like almonds.
5 When in doubt, don't touch, and certainly don't eat plants you can't identify.

Deadly amphibian

The golden poison arrow frog of South and Central America contains enough poison to kill 10,000 mice! Forest people tip their darts and arrows in the poison so even a scratch is lethal.

Bees, wasps and ants

Tropical species can be large and aggressive. Their stings can trigger an allergic reaction that could be fatal. If you disturb a bee or wasp nest, the best advice is to run! On the trail, take great care not to dislodge insect nests in trees.

➡ Paper wasps of the tropics build large nests of chewed wood fibres.

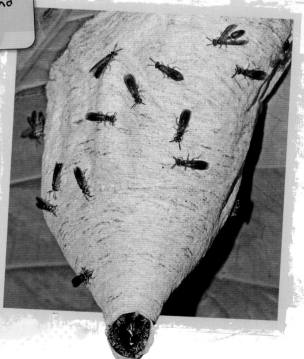

IDENTIFYING POISONOUS CREATURES

Many jungle animals can inflict painful bites and stings, some deadly. A quick look at the appearance can identify the species, but keep well away.

Scorpions

These hard-bodied creatures have eight legs, large front claws and a curving sting on the tail. Stings are usually painful rather than dangerous.

Centipedes

These many-legged creatures are nocturnal hunters. Tropical species reach 30 cm long. Bites are painful rather than dangerous.

Goliath tarantula

These large, hairy spiders grow to 28 cm across. The venom is fairly mild but they can shoot hairs that irritate the skin.

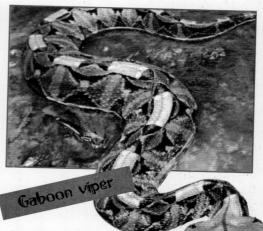

Gaboon viper

This African snake grows to 2 m long. The brown-and-black markings provide excellent camouflage. It is deadly poisonous.

WOW!

English traveller Mary Kingsley explored West Africa in the 1890s. She estimated that 75 percent of jungle insects stung, five percent bit, and the rest were parasites!

Perilous waters

DEADLY PERIL LURKS in rivers, lakes and swamps in the jungle. Aquatic terrors include flesh-eating piranhas, huge snakes and terrifying crocodiles. Make sure you know what's in the water before you enter or approach.

⬇ Watch out for crocodiles when washing or collecting water from a river.

Crocs and relatives

Crocodiles, alligators and caimans infest tropical wetlands. These huge reptiles, measuring up to 5 m, are powerful swimmers and surprisingly fast on land. They lurk submerged with just their eyes showing. They seize unwary animals that come to drink, drag them underwater and hold them there until they drown.

Beware the anaconda

This snake of the Amazon River grows to 7.5 m in length. It wraps its coils around its prey, then tightens its grip. The victim dies of suffocation or drowning. An adult snake is big and powerful enough to kill a caiman and swallow it whole.

➡ Anacondas feed on rodents, pigs, tapirs, deer, water birds, frogs and other reptiles.

NOTES

GET READY

Preparation and equipment

Planning your trip

PREPARATION IS KEY to jungle survival. This includes careful planning and getting the right equipment. Research the area you plan to visit thoroughly and hone your survival skills. That way, even if you are stranded, you will have the skills and knowledge to survive.

Laying plans

Plan every stage of the expedition in detail. Divide the trip into three stages: the journey in, the expedition, and the return to civilization. The length of your trip will affect the food and equipment you take. You will also need a backup plan in case things go wrong – for example if one of your group gets sick or injured, if bad weather strikes, or if a vehicle breaks down.

⬇ Study a local map to get to know the region thoroughly before you go.

⬇ Make a checklist of supplies and potential problems you could encounter on each stage of your journey.

	Journey in	Expedition	Journey home
Date			
Estimated time			
Documents required			
Route			
Likely hazards/problems			
Food			
Equipment			
Clothing			
Medical supplies			

TIP

Leave details of your trip with a friend or family. If possible, give grid references for your location every day. Update the person if your plans change during the trip.

Expedition kit

HAVING THE RIGHT KIT IS VITAL to the success of a jungle trip. Think about the gear you will need by day and night, on the move and while camping. Deciding what to take is a balancing act. Take too little, and you may miss out an essential item. **Take too much and you will weigh yourself down.**

Must-have items

A map and compass, and firelighting and signalling kits are essential. Other must-haves include a head torch, water purifying tablets or iodine, and a mosquito net. A space blanket or tarpaulin provide shelter in an emergency.

Mirror

Headtorch

Whistle

Mobile phone

Compass

Maps

GPS (global positioning system)

Matches

Mosquito net

Laser flare

Space blanket

Fire steel

Mini survival kit

Lighter

➡ A mini survival kit could save your life. It should include things such as a penknife, safety pins, a torch, a candle, and a repair kit such as needle and thread.

→ The blade of a folding knife slots safely into the handle.

Useful knives

Cutting equipment is essential. Although a penknife is useful, the blade is too small for cutting wood. A folding knife is good for bushcraft. You will need a machete to hack your way through the jungle. Stow it in a sheath when not in use. Keep hands away from sharp cutting edges and always take care when handling knives.

← A machete is a must for moving through jungle and making camp. Take great care when swinging a machete if your group is moving single-file.

→ Multi-tools have useful attachments such as pliers, a tin-opener and scissors.

TRY THIS AT HOME   USING A COMPASS

Knowing how to use a compass is vital in the jungle, where there are few landmarks and you can rarely see far ahead. The red floating compass needle always points north. This gives you the four basic directions: north, south, east and west. Practise using these bearings on a playing field. Take 20 paces north, then turn (and without looking up) take 20 paces west, then south and finally east. This should take you to the exact point you began.

↑ The lid of this folding compass protects the dial from damage.

BEFORE YOU LEAVE

1 Check all your gear is in working order.

2 Read instructions on new equipment to make sure you know how to use it.

3 Take spares of vital kit such as an extra torch and matches.

4 Stow kit in plastic bags to protect from moisture. Cloth bags help you to sort your gear.

Dress for the jungle

LIGHTWEIGHT CLOTHING that dries quickly is a must on jungle trips. The hot, sticky conditions will make you long to strip off, but you need to keep your whole body covered to guard against insects, leeches and other pests.

What to wear

Jungle clothing should be made of cotton, or artificial fabrics that wick away sweat. Take cotton underwear, long-sleeved shirts and t-shirts, and loose-fitting trousers. A wide-brimmed hat, sunglasses and bandana will complete your outfit. Jungle boots have rubber soles with deep treads. Boots with canvas uppers dry quickly after a soaking. High boots will guard against leeches.

A t-shirt and bandana will help to absorb sweat

Keep trousers and socks tucked into boots to keep leeches and mosquitoes out

Trousers should be made of a lightweight, quick-drying material

TIP
Don't take jeans. While the fabric is tough, it soaks up moisture and dries very slowly.

Wide-brimmed hat guards against sunstroke

TIP

Keep a set of dry clothes in a plastic bag. At the end of the day, take off your wet clothes and put on comfy dry clothing. Dry the wet set overnight.

➡ Wash clothes as soon as you make camp to maximize drying time.

WOW!

Spanish adventurer Gonzalo Pizarro led an Amazon expedition in the 1500s. A writer, Inca de La Vega, reported: "On account of the constant waters from above and below, they were always wet, and their clothes rotted, so that they had to go naked."

Washing clothes

Damp, sweaty clothing quickly develops mildew and starts to rot. Wash clothes to remove grime and sweat at the end of the day, and dry them by the fire or in the sun. Take travel wash or a small bag of soap powder and clothes pegs. Use string to rig a washing line between trees.

Packing your gear

A tough rucksack will hold all your gear, and you will need a waterproof rucksack cover. Pack less vital kit at the bottom, with items you will need first on top. Stow essential kit such as water bottle, documents, map and compass in the side pockets. Check that all your gear fits inside your rucksack.

Sturdy, lightweight rucksack with plenty of storage

Straps at the top hold rolled camping mat

Keep water bottle upright to guard against leaks

Sleeping bag packs away small

Food and medicine

THE RATIONS YOU TAKE on your trip should provide a balanced diet to keep you fit and healthy. You must also pack a first aid kit and learn how to deal with minor injuries along the way.

FOOD AND THE BODY'S NEEDS

Food provides the energy you need for action and to maintain body heat. A balanced diet includes protein, carbohydrates, fats and fibre. Vitamins and minerals help the body repair injuries and fight illness.

Sugar provides a quick energy fix in an emergency

Fibre in fresh fruit and vegetables helps digestion. Many jungle fruits are edible, but you need to be sure what you are eating

Protein in meat, fish, eggs and nuts builds bones and muscles. In an emergency, insects, grubs and worms provide protein

Carbohydrates in rice, pasta and bread provide energy

Expedition food

Take a variety of foods in watertight containers. Dried, canned and powdered foods last longer than fresh foods, but canned foods are heavy. You will need salt to replace the salt you lose as you sweat. If you intend to eat local foods you will need a handbook or a local guide to show you what is edible and what is not.

← Canned foods such as beans and sardines keep well.

→ Not only does a hot meal provide nutrients, it also boosts morale.

Mess kit

To boil water, prepare food and eat it you will need a cooking pan, plate, mug, cutlery, can opener, chopping board and dishtowel.

First aid kit

A medical kit to treat injuries is vital. You will also need malaria tablets, painkillers, travel sickness pills and antihistamines for insect bites. Pack a first aid manual or better still, go on a first aid course.

→ Keep your medical kit in a watertight container to avoid mould and bug attack.

TIP

Before you go, you will need to have vaccinations for the tropics. Contact your doctor's surgery well in advance.

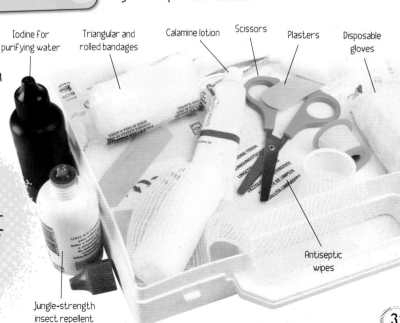

Iodine for purifying water

Triangular and rolled bandages

Calamine lotion

Scissors

Plasters

Disposable gloves

Antiseptic wipes

Jungle-strength insect repellent

31

AMAZON SCIENTIST
Alexander von Humboldt

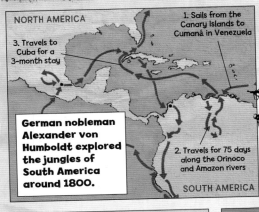

NORTH AMERICA

3. Travels to Cuba for a 3-month stay

1. Sails from the Canary Islands to Cumaná in Venezuela

German nobleman Alexander von Humboldt explored the jungles of South America around 1800.

2. Travels for 75 days along the Orinoco and Amazon rivers

SOUTH AMERICA

He was an expert geographer and naturalist. In the summer of 1799 he set sail from France with botanist Aimé Bonpland.

Starting from Caracas, they travelled south until they reached the Apure, a tributary of the Orinoco River. There they saw pink river dolphins.

They journeyed by canoe down the Orinoco. Following its course they discovered that the Casiquiare River connected the vast river systems of the Amazon and the Orinoco. The waters were infested with crocs.

For the next few weeks, they trekked through dense jungle. Swarms of mosquitoes and stifling heat made the going tough. Eventually, their food was destroyed by insects and rain. All they had to eat were ground-up cacao beans and river water.

In 1804, the men returned to civilization. Von Humboldt was invited to meet President Jefferson in the United States, and the pair became friends.

NOTES

GET SAFE

Basic survival skills

First things first

YOUR BASIC SURVIVAL NEEDS are water, food, fire and shelter. In any survival situation, these needs are top priority. In an emergency, keep calm. The most important thing is to get yourself out of danger. Treat any injuries. Then think about your position. **Weigh up whether it's best to move or stay put.**

Organize rations

Try to establish how long the food you have will last. Plan a daily menu that will give you a balanced diet. If supplies are low, you will need to add to your rations by living off the land.

⬇ A local guide prepares food in the Peruvian jungle.

TIP
Do not scratch mosquito bites. They will only itch more, and you risk getting them infected.

Mosquito protection

Mosquitoes can transmit not only malaria, but deadly dengue fever and yellow fever. Arrange mosquito netting over your hat at dawn and dusk. Apply jungle-strength insect repellent, but don't use it near your eyes or on your forehead, where sweat might wash it into your eyes. If you don't have repellent, mud can help to deter insects from biting exposed skin.

⬅ Mosquitoes will bite any area of exposed skin. Cover up as much as you can.

Vital water

WATER IS YOUR BODY'S number one need. You can survive for several weeks without food, but you can only last a few days without water. Water is generally abundant in jungles, but you must purify it. Collect rainwater or use water from a fast-flowing stream.

The body and water

Water is essential to keep your body in working order. You need to drink at least 2–3 litres a day to replace water lost through sweating, breathing and urinating. In hot conditions you may need 10 litres or more.

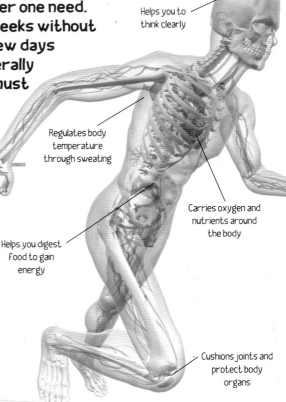

Helps you to think clearly

Regulates body temperature through sweating

Carries oxygen and nutrients around the body

Helps you digest food to gain energy

Cushions joints and protect body organs

COLLECTING RAINWATER

Rig a tarpaulin between branches to catch rainwater. Weigh it down with a stone to channel water into a container, positioned below to catch the drips. Make sure you skim any bugs off the surface before you drink.

➡ A basic water collector is simple to set up.

Use a stone to weigh down the tarp

Container catches water

MAKE A WATER FILTER

You can make a basic water filter from a plastic bottle, string, and coarse and fine rocky materials such as sand and gravel. Boil or treat the water after filtering before you drink it.

1   Cut the bottom off the bottle. Turn it upside down and tie a cloth or sock over the neck.

2   Put a layer of fine sand at the bottom, then coarse sand. Next comes fine gravel, with coarse gravel on top.

3   Make two holes at the top of the bottle, thread string through and hang the filter from a branch.

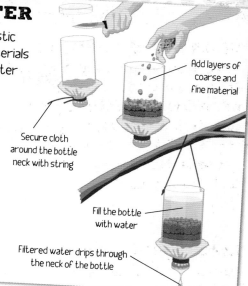

Add layers of coarse and fine material

Secure cloth around the bottle neck with string

Fill the bottle with water

Filtered water drips through the neck of the bottle

WOW!

Animals could lead you to drinking water. Plant-eaters are rarely far from water, which they drink mostly at dawn and sunset.

WATER DOS AND DON'TS

1   Boil all water for at least ten minutes to kill germs.
2   Never drink salty water.
3   Cup-shaped pitcher plants and bromeliads hold rainwater.
4   Conserve water by working slowly.
5   Take small sips — gulping could make you choke.

➡ Don't let the vine touch your mouth, as it may have irritant hairs.

Water-holding vines

Hollow vines may contain water. Look for a long vine about 5 cm in diameter. Reach up as high as you can and cut a deep notch in the vine. If the liquid that seeps out is milky, don't drink it. Cut the stem close to the ground and collect the liquid in a container. When it stops dripping, cut the vine higher up to get more water.

Temporary shelter

AN EMERGENCY SHELTER will keep you and your kit dry – a top priority. In the jungle you need to sleep off the ground, well away from biting insects, spiders and centipedes. You will need a few hours to build a shelter. **Don't leave It too late to make camp.**

BASIC SHELTER

1 Lash the ends of two branches together with rope. Stand them up to make an A-frame. Lash the frame to a small tree or stout branch to provide support.

2 Lash two more branches to make a second A-frame. Line it up about 2 m from the first. If possible, add a guy rope for support.

3 Place a lighter pole across the two to form a ridgepole.

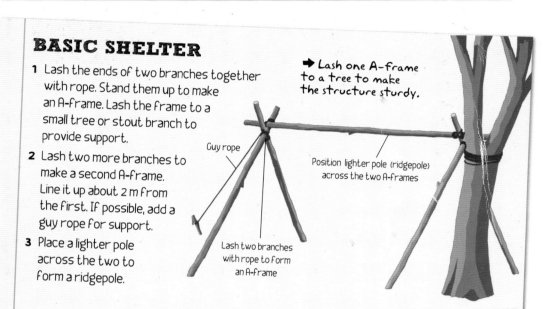

➡ Lash one A-frame to a tree to make the structure sturdy.

Guy rope

Position lighter pole (ridgepole) across the two A-frames

Lash two branches with rope to form an A-frame

CAMP BED

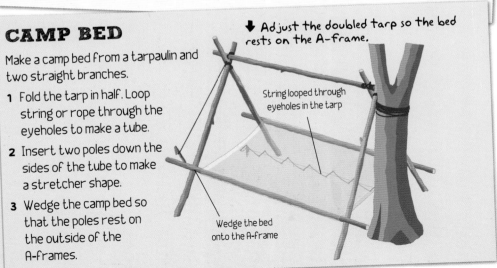

⬇ Adjust the doubled tarp so the bed rests on the A-frame.

Make a camp bed from a tarpaulin and two straight branches.

1 Fold the tarp in half. Loop string or rope through the eyeholes to make a tube.

2 Insert two poles down the sides of the tube to make a stretcher shape.

3 Wedge the camp bed so that the poles rest on the outside of the A-frames.

String looped through eyeholes in the tarp

Wedge the bed onto the A-frame

40

TARPAULIN ROOF

Complete the shelter by rigging a tarpaulin over the top of the A-frame. Secure the tarp with guy ropes at each corner, tied to branches or pegs in the ground. Keep the tarp away from the A-frame, it should only touch the ridgepole at the top.

Guy ropes

➡ Use a stone to drive pegs or stakes into the ground.

Pegs made from sharpened sticks

Making fire

A FIRE IS A MUST for survival. It gives light, keeps you warm and dries clothing. It allows you to boil water, cook food and signal for help. It keeps insects and larger animals away. However, damp jungle conditions make it hard to light a fire.

WHAT YOU NEED

A fire has four key ingredients:

Tinder

Dry material that lights easily, such as paper, wood shavings, dry grass, moss or bark.

Kindling

Small, dry twigs help to get the fire going

Fuel

Logs and branches feed the fire. Some can be damp. Collect lots of fuel to keep the fire going.

TIP

Beware of insects, snakes and centipedes when gathering fallen wood.

Means of lighting

Matches, a lighter or firesteel.

MAKE FEATHERSTICKS

Five or six feathersticks will help you light a fire. You need dryish sticks and a knife.

1. Remove the bark and any damp wood. Holding the blade at an angle, run your knife down the stick to make shavings.

2. Turn the stick slightly and repeat. Work around the stick. Use any shavings that drop off for kindling.

Always work the knife away from your body

➡ Brace the stick against a board or flat tree-stump.

BUILD A FIRE PLATFORM

Site your fire on dry ground if possible, not too close to your shelter. A fire platform will get your fire off damp ground.

1 Cut four sticks about 60 cm long. Trim the ends at an angle. Drive them into the ground to form a square.

2 Cut four more sticks of similar length and lash them to the tops of the first four sticks, to finish the square.

3 Place green sticks or logs on top of the square to make a platform. Cover with a layer of earth.

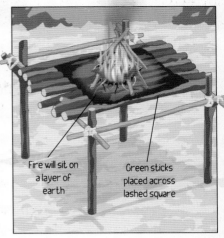

Fire will sit on a layer of earth

Green sticks placed across lashed square

WARNING!

Fires are very dangerous. Have water standing by to douse the fire if necessary.

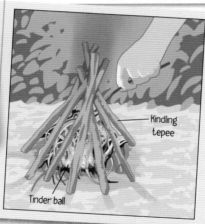

Kindling tepee

Tinder ball

LAY AND LIGHT A FIRE

1 Clear space in which to make the fire. Place a ball of tinder in the middle.

2 Build a teepee shape of kindling over the tinder.

3 Light the tinder. As the kindling burns add more fuel – small twigs at first.

Sustaining your fire

Keep your fire going overnight by covering it with ashes. Place one or two large logs on top. In the morning, poke the ashes with a stick and add kindling. Always make sure your fire is completely out before you move on.

➜ A fire provides a welcome morale boost first thing in the morning.

Organizing camp

SURVIVAL IS ALL ABOUT using energy efficiently. Keeping your camp and gear neat and tidy will stop you losing things, which wastes energy. **It's vital to keep your food and equipment safe and dry.**

Divide tasks

On a group expedition, you need to divide tasks between people to work efficiently. You could either match tasks to group members' skills, or make a rota so jobs change daily. Make sure everyone does his or her fair share of chores such as collecting water, feeding the fire and gathering wood.

← Make a checklist of tasks to divide among the group. Everyone needs a responsibility.

TIP
Protect your food supplies by replacing lids on containers. Check stock regularly to make sure damp and/or insects haven't got in.

Protect your gear

Steamy, wet rainforest conditions can damage equipment, so make sure you look after it. Don't leave equipment lying around where it could get wet, as metal tools such as knives will soon become rusty. Always make sure vital kit such as matches and dry clothing are kept dry in plastic bags. Put tools back in the right place when you have finished using them. While working, watch where you put tools down, so they don't get lost.

↑ At night, put your boots upside-down on sticks to prevent bugs crawling in.

LOST IN THE AMAZON
Loïc Pillois and Guilhem Nayral

In 2007, two Frenchmen, Loïc Pillois and Guilhem Nayral, planned a 125-km hike through remote jungle in French Guyana. From a drop point on the Approuague River, they planned to head west to the town of Saül.

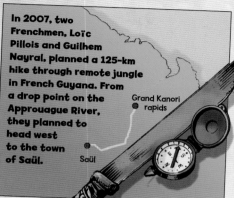

Grand Kanori rapids

Saül

The men set out with a map, compass, machetes, tarp, hammocks, and enough food for 12 days. They made slow progress, due to the need to hack their way through dense jungle with machetes.

On day 12 they knew they were in trouble. Saül lay in a valley, but the way west led upwards. They were lost and out of food.

They decided to make camp, knowing that a rescue would be launched.

They rigged the tarp to keep the rain off, and built a fire, hoping that it would attract a search party...

...But the dense forest canopy hid the smoke, and though they heard helicopters, rescue never came.

The men survived on centipedes, beetles, grubs and palm seeds. They ate small amounts of unfamiliar plants to see if they were edible.

They also caught tarantulas, which they cooked to neutralize the poison.

Cont. ➡

After three weeks, the men thought the rescue had been called off.

They decided they would have to walk out. So they headed west, but were too weak to walk for more than three hours a day.

Swamps blocked their route. A week later, they caught a turtle, which they cooked and ate – claws and all. They heated the blood and drank it – they said it tasted amazing!

The next day Nayral caught another spider, but didn't cook it long enough to neutralize the poison. His mouth and tongue swelled up and went numb.

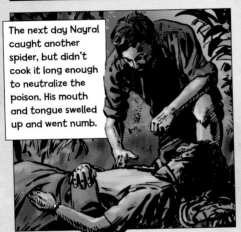

Greatly weakened and in terrible pain, Nayral could not continue to walk. Convinced that Saül must be close, Pillois left his friend and pushed on.

Pillois finally reached Saül. Exhausted, he flagged down help and and raised the alarm.

Thirty-six hours later, a helicopter found Nayral and lifted him to safety. It turned out the men had made their final camp just 4 km from Saül! Both men made a full recovery.

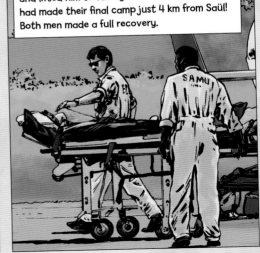

NOTES

GET SETTLED

Advanced camp skills

Camp craft

IF YOU MEAN TO STAY a while in the jungle, you will need a proper camp, so build a better shelter and try your hand at finding local foods. You can use your bushcraft skills to make tools and gadgets that will **make camp life more comfortable**.

KEY

1 Hang food rations on a low branch, away from the trunk and main branches, to keep from predators

2 Latrine should be downwind of camp and downstream from water source

3 Pitch your camp near a source of wood

4 Dig a small run-off trench around your shelter to reduce risk of flooding

5 Locate nearby water source

6 Build three signal fires on open ground

7 Assign open areas for location aids and as a landing site for a rescue helicopter

Siting a permanent camp

Take time to select a campsite that provides protection from the weather. Choose a site near water, but not on the valley floor or in a deep gully, which could prove a death trap after heavy rain. Never camp across an animal trail – you never know what will come wandering through!

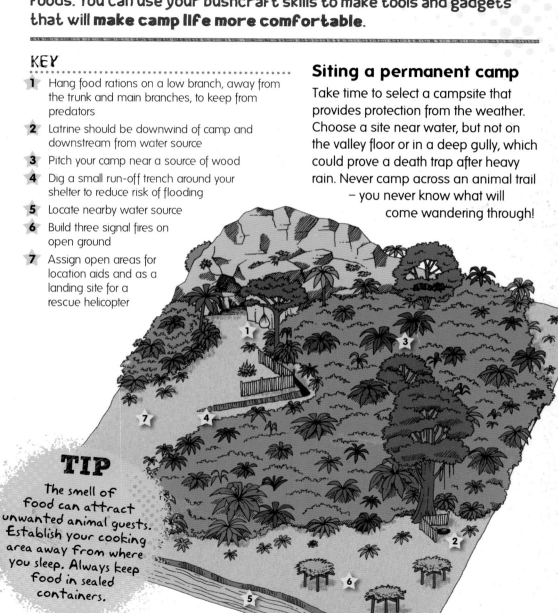

TIP

The smell of food can attract unwanted animal guests. Establish your cooking area away from where you sleep. Always keep food in sealed containers.

Bushcraft skills

THE SKILLS YOU NEED to survive in the wild are known as bushcraft. They include tracking, navigating and using natural materials to make things. Developing bushcraft skills will make your jungle stay more comfortable and keep you in good spirits.

BUILD A FIRE REFLECTOR

This wooden screen will deflect warmth from the fire into your shelter, and also protect the fire from gusts of wind.

1 Cut four wooden stakes. Shave the ends into points and drive two stakes into the ground, a pole's width apart.
2 Position the other pair of stakes parallel to the first as shown. Pile straightish sticks into the frame.
3 Stuff the cracks with mud or leaves. Tie the stakes at the top.

Steps 1 and 2

Add sticks to the frame

← A firescreen maximizes the heat your fire provides.

Step 3

Mud to fill cracks

MAKE SOME ROPE

String and rope, known as cordage, can be made using long, stringy plant stems. Take two stems and roll them between your palms to twist the fibres. Repeat to make a second strand. Tie one end and secure it. Twist the strands in the opposite direction to join them together. Three strands plaited together will be even stronger. New strands can be woven in to make a longer cord.

↑ Grasses, slender vines, palm tree leaves and animal hair can all be used to make rope.

Lashings

Rope or string can be tied in different ways to help build shelters, rafts and many other objects. Square lashing is used to join poles in a cross. Diagonal lashing is used to bind poles at an angle, for example to make an A-frame.

TIP

Jungle vines and wild honeysuckle make good cordage. Soak before using to make them flexible.

TRY THIS AT HOME — HOW TO USE LASHINGS

Square lashing

1 Hold the poles in position. Tie a knot around the bottom strut.

2 Wind string or rope over and under the poles, pulling it tight each time.

3 Twist it right around one strut and wind in the opposite direction.

4 Secure with a tight knot.

Diagonal lashing

1 Tie a knot around one pole. Bind the poles loosely.

2 Then loop rope or string between the poles, around the binding.

3 Loop the rope between the poles four or five times.

4 Pull tight and secure with a knot.

BUILD A COOKING TRIPOD

Make a cooking tripod for the fire by lashing three poles together. Newly cut green wood is best to use. Use wire, rope or string to hang a pot or kettle over the fire. You could also make a rack for cooking fish and meat.

1 Splay the sticks to form a tripod. Tie the top with cord using the diagonal lashing method.

2 Make a cooking rack by weaving sticks or tying them together. Wedge it onto the tripod.

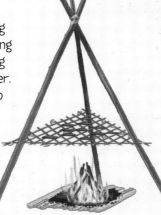

What's on the menu?

IF RATIONS ARE RUNNING LOW you will need to try local foods. Bugs could be on the menu if you aren't squeamish. Fruit, nuts, roots, shoots, and berries are plentiful, but you need to positively identify everything. Eating the wrong food will cause stomach cramps and at worst, **could be fatal**.

TOP JUNGLE FOODS

Many jungle foods are nourishing. If you're unsure of a food's identity, try a tiny amount on your lips and then your tongue. If there is any stinging or numbness, spit it out.

Palm hearts

The soft tips of young palm stems. Access by chopping the top off a young palm tree.

Bamboo

The young shoots of this rapidly sprouting plant can be eaten.

Banana

The young shoots of this familiar fruit are also edible. Cook the green fruit.

Mango

This delicious large-stoned fruit grows on evergreen trees.

Coconut

This palm tree nut contains a refreshing drink and tasty food. Pierce the soft 'eye' with a knife to drink, then crack open to eat.

← Palm hearts are edible if you strip off the outer layers.

One bug or two?

Insects, slugs and earthworms are a great source of protein in an emergency. Look for woodboring grubs under bark. Remove the wings of large insects such as crickets. Worms and maggots (fly larvae) are safe to eat raw or cooked. It's best to roast or boil beetles to kill parasites. Avoid brightly coloured insects, hairy caterpillars and minibeasts that sting.

⬆ Witchetty grubs are a delicacy in Australian jungles. These giant grubs have a nutty flavour and provide a high-protein meal.

WOW!

In the 1500s, Spaniard Francisco de Orellana led a boat trip down the Amazon. When food ran out, the men were left with "nothing to eat except the skins that formed their girdles, and the leather of their shoes, boiled up with a few herbs."

⬆ A Yanomami Indian fills a fine mesh basket with grated cassava to wring out the moisture. Mashed cassava is then used to make flour and bread.

Poisonous food

Many rainforest peoples clear patches of jungle to grow crops such as cassava. This root contains deadly cyanide, so the tubers have to be soaked, grated, squeezed and then sieved to remove the poison. The pulp is then made into a porridge and baked on the fire.

TIP

Don't take chances when eating fruit. If in doubt, watch what monkeys and parrots are eating. Any fruit that is eaten by monkeys is probably safe for humans too.

Jungle-style fishing

RAINFOREST HUNTERS regularly bring meat home for their families. Arrows and blowpipe darts are used to shoot game down from the treetops, but you need to be an expert shot. Fishing is a far better bet than hunting if you are hungry and **need a nutritious meal**.

Fishing tackle

If you don't have a fishing line, use string, or even spare bootlaces if necessary. Bent safety pins, wire or thorns make excellent hooks. Worms, slugs, insects, bread or berries can be used as bait. Try different baits and see what works best. If you tie your line to a stick to make a fishing rod, you can cast further out.

← Live worms provide a tempting lure for fish.

TIP
Fish are attracted to light. If you have a torch, try shining it at the water's surface in the evening. As fish come to the surface, kill them using the flat side of your machete.

MAKE A FISHING SPEAR

You need a strong but slender length of bamboo about 1.8 m long. Use a knife to make a cross-shaped cut in one end.

1 The cuts should extend about 15 cm down the shaft.

2 Push string or vine between the prongs to separate them. Sharpen the prongs with a knife.

3 Bind string around the shaft so the bamboo doesn't split further.

A Pinare Indian squats by a stream with spear poised, waiting for a fish.

WOW!

Amazon tribes use poison from the shilashila vine to catch fish. Bundles of this deadly vine are pounded and trodden underfoot in a canoe. This concentrates the poison, which is then tipped into the water to kill and paralyze fish.

Successful fishing

Jungle fish hide in deep shady pools by day, so dawn and dusk are good times to go fishing. Stand on a rock or in the water, with your spear tip close to the surface. Stay quiet and still, and be patient. When a fish comes into range, thrust your spear forwards to pin it to the bottom. You can also turn over rocks to find crabs and shrimps.

Cooking the catch

Fish will spoil quickly so you need to eat it fresh. Slit the belly and remove the guts, which make great bait. Remove the head and tail unless the fish is tiny. Beware of catfish, which have sharp spines. If you have it, cook the fish in foil in the ashes of your fire. Alternatively, fry it in a pan or roast on a spit.

Fish roasted on spits is both delicious and nutritious.

Advanced shelters

A WATERTIGHT SHELTER will help you get a good night's sleep, which is important for health and well-being. A raised sleeping platform will lift you out of reach of creepy-crawlies, giving peace of mind during the night.

MAKE A PALM FROND SHELTER

1 Build the framework

You need four sturdy uprights. At least one should be a living tree if possible. Cut stakes about 2 m long. Sharpen the ends and drive them into the ground to form a rectangle about 2.5 by 2 m. Lash cross struts to the uprights about one metre off the ground.

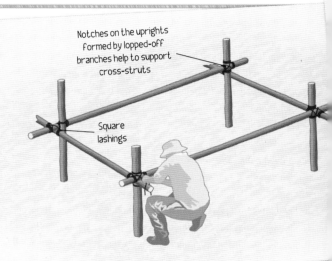

Notches on the uprights formed by lopped-off branches help to support cross-struts

Square lashings

Local materials

Rainforest peoples use local materials to build shelters. Fast-growing bamboo stems make stout poles, but you have to be careful of sharp splinters. Vines, rattan or handmade string is used for binding. Large banana leaves and palm fronds make great thatch.

← A Baka pygmy of West Africa pegs leaves onto a round framework to make a hut.

58

2 Add the roof

Lean four long, straight branches across the uprights to form two A-frames. Sharpen the ends and push them into the ground. Lash the tops and add a ridgepole. Lash on lighter cross-struts. Use large leaves to make a thatched roof.

3 Make the sleeping platform

Lash a framework of lighter poles onto the support poles. Pile on springy branches. Weave in leaves and straw to make a comfy mattress.

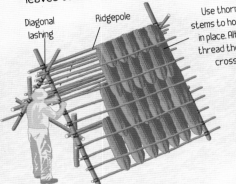

Diagonal lashing

Ridgepole

Use thorns or leaf stems to hold the leaves in place. Alternatively, thread them onto the cross struts.

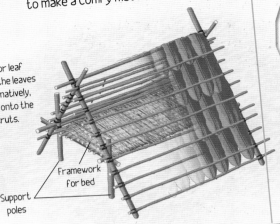

Framework for bed

Support poles

TIP
Dig a trench around your shelter to drain rainwater and deter creepy-crawlies. Any bugs that fall into the trench can be eaten or used as bait!

Hygiene around water

A few simple ground rules on hygiene will keep your camp clean and healthy. Draw water from the river upstream of camp. You can wash yourself near camp, but wash clothes and dishes downstream. The toilet area should be a short distance from your shelter, well away from water.

➡ Washing your hands before preparing food is particularly important in the tropics.

JUNGLE HIDEOUT
Shoichi Yokoi

Yokoi was a Japanese soldier during World War II (1939–45). In 1943 he was stationed on the Pacific island of Guam. As the war ended, US forces occupied Guam.

Rather than surrender, which was considered dishonourable, Yokoi escaped into the jungle along with nine other soldiers.

Yokoi lived on fruit, snails and coconuts. He caught eels and shrimps in the river. He used wire to make a rat trap and drew river water or collected rainwater in bamboo tubes, always boiling it before drinking.

A tailor by trade, Yokoi made clothes using tree bark. He beat the bark into thin sheets, which he sewed with a handmade needle.

Towards the end of his ordeal, Yokoi lived in an underground cave that he had dug with a makeshift trowel. It was lit by an oil lamp made from coconut shells.

Yokoi made fire using a flashlight lens and later by rubbing sticks together. He kept an ember burning on a coconut-fibre rope.

In 1972, two hunters on the island found Yokoi – he had been hiding in the jungle for 28 years! He was returned to Japan and became a national hero.

Doctors declared Yokoi in good health. He went back to Japan and married, then returned to Guam for his honeymoon. He died in 1997, aged 82.

NOTES

61

GET MOVING

Movement and navigation

Moving on

MOVING THROUGH DENSE JUNGLE is never easy. You need to be an expert navigator to make your way through featureless forest. You must be skilled with a machete, and ready to wade or raft across rivers. **One false move could be your last!**

Stay or go?

If you are stranded by accident, you may need to hike to safety. But first stop, and weigh up all the options. Are you injured? Will a search party come looking for you? If so, you should probably stay put. If no one knows where you are and you cannot signal for help, you may have to move.

← Hikers move through dense terrain in the Amazon jungle.

CHECK OUT THE TERRAIN

Take a close look at a map before you go, to investigate what lies ahead. Check the key to find out how cliffs, gorges, scree, marshes and other features are shown. Study the courses of rivers. Make sure you know how bridges and settlements are shown – they could be your passport to safety.

→ Careful studying of the terrain on your route can shave hours, or days, off your journey.

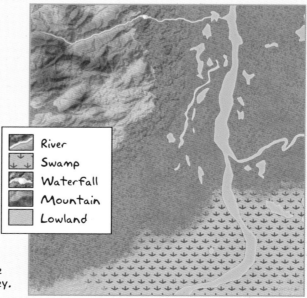

River
Swamp
Waterfall
Mountain
Lowland

Get prepared

IF YOU DECIDE TO MOVE ON, make thorough preparations first. Hone your map and compass skills. Work out the route, and divide it into manageable stages. Pack carefully so you **don't end up lugging too much weight**.

Map scales and distance

Maps are drawn to different scales. On a 1:25,000 map, 4 cm on the map represents 1 km on the ground. On a 1:50,000 map, 2 cm is 1 km. If the map has a grid, each square is one unit of distance. Use the grid to estimate distance, and the time you will need to cover it. On easy terrain you can walk 4 km/h, but progress is much slower in the jungle.

➡ A small-scale map (top-left) shows a large area such as the Amazon Basin in less detail. A large-scale map (bottom-right) shows a smaller area in greater detail.

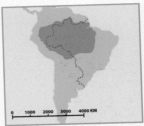
Scale: 1 cm = 2000 km

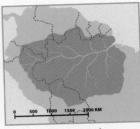
Scale: 1 cm = 1000 km

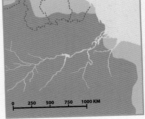
Scale: 1 cm = 250 km

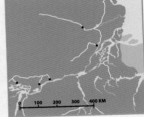
Scale: 1 cm = 200 km

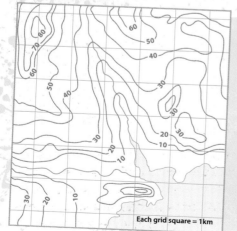
Each grid square = 1km

Working with contours

Contour lines on a map show the height above sea level. Heights are also marked in figures. To work out the height of a climb, subtract the figure marked in the valley from the height at the top. Where the contours lie close together, the climb is steep.

⬅ On a flat map, contour lines show how steep the landscape is.

A compass is vital for navigation. If you don't have one, make one using a magnet and a needle. Stroke the needle over the magnet many times in one direction. Then move the magnet a safe distance away so it doesn't attract the needle. Float the magnetized needle on a leaf in still water. It will settle pointing north-south. Use the sun to get your general bearings, so you know which way is north. The sun rises in the east and sets in the west.

⬇ Keep all metal away from the floating needle, as this can interfere with how it moves.

Magnet

Plastic container

WOW!

Mbayaka pygmies of West Africa carry fire on a journey by wrapping a burning ember in bracket fungus. The fungus is wrapped in green leaves. When they stop, they blow on the ember to make instant fire.

⬇ When travelling in a group, move in single file, following the leader's track.

TIP

Pack only what you need for your journey. Decide if each item is really necessary. Unnecessary kit will slow you down and tire you out, making you less likely to spot danger.

Your trusty staff

Cut a staff for your jungle hike. A stick will provide support on uneven ground and save wear and tear on the knees when heading downhill. Use it to part vegetation and dislodge lurking minibeasts. You can also use it to fend away thorns and test marshy ground.

Finding the way

NAVIGATION CAN BE A NIGHTMARE in dense forest. When every tree looks the same, it's incredibly easy to get disorientated. Luckily your compass and map skills will help **keep you on track**.

Survey the route

Before you set off, try to survey the terrain from a high point. A cliff, hill or tree may provide a view across the jungle. Notice features such as hills and rivers. Is there any sign of civilization? Take time to locate the same features on your map, and work out the easiest route.

← Keeping a straight course is difficult when moving over very rough ground.

SETTING THE MAP

Setting the map means using a map and compass to find your direction.

Direction arrow

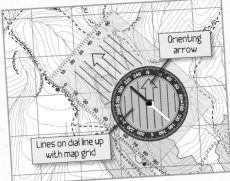

Orienting arrow

Lines on dial line up with map grid

1 Place the edge of your compass on the map along the route you want to travel, with the direction arrow pointing the way forward.

2 Turn the rotating dial so the north-south lines on the dial line up with the map grid. Make sure the orienting arrow on the dial points north.

Maintaining a bearing

Dense growth, treetrunks and roots make it hard to stay on course. If there are several people in your party, send a 'scout' ahead on the bearing. Stay within hearing. Catch up with the scout and send him or her on again. If you are on your own, fix your eyes on a tree ahead. When you reach it, look back to get your bearings. Then look ahead, and fix on another tree.

← A local guide scouts the easiest route through dense undergrowth in the Amazon.

Making a detour

If you meet an obstacle such as a cliff or crag, you may have to detour around it. Keep on the bearing by using your compass to make four 90-degree turns. Count the number of paces you make on stage 1. Make the same number of paces on stage 3, and you'll be back on track again.

TIP

If you are completely lost, find a stream or river and head downstream. Most settlements are located on rivers, so sooner or later you should reach civilization.

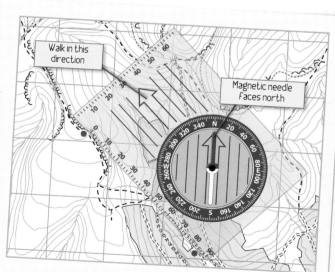

Walk in this direction

Magnetic needle faces north

3 Hold the map level and turn your body until the magnetic needle of the compass faces north. The direction arrow now gives your bearing – where you want to go.

↑ Before you cross a stream, note a landmark marking your onward direction on the opposite bank.

On the trail

JUNGLE TRAVEL IS HOT, sweaty and exhausting. Take frequent rests and keep drinking water. Don't overestimate the distance you can cover – and **don't leave it too late in the day to make camp**.

Using a machete

Clear only enough vegetation to move forwards. Chop downwards and sideways, so the growth falls away from the path. Chop bamboo to the ground – don't leave tall spikes that could injure people following. Using a machete is tiring. When in a group, keep changing the lead person who is clearing the route.

➡ Keep your machete sharp, and dry it after use, or it will rust.

WARNING!

If you are leading a group and using a machete, be careful that your backswing does not injure anyone behind you.

Danger all around

Keep your eyes peeled for danger ahead, such as snakes coiled around branches. Take animal trails only if they lead the way you want to go, or you could end up going in circles. Cut a notch in a tree now and then, to mark the route you have taken. This will make it easier to backtrack if necessary. Remember to stop often and check for ticks and leeches.

⬅ Beware of following in the tracks of predators such as mountain lions. Look out for dung or scratch marks on trees.

TROUBLESOME TERRAIN

Jungle vegetation is extremely dense, and this makes it difficult to see far ahead. It can also conceal natural hazards.

Thick foliage

TIP

Pick up dry tinder you see on the trail. Bag it for later to light a fire when you make camp.

This can conceal cliffs, crags and gorges until you are almost on top of them. Look through the vegetation, not at it, to spot danger ahead.

Cliffs and gorges

Steep slopes

Never drop over an overhanging slab without checking what lies beyond. Face inwards when climbing sheer rock faces. Use a rope to scale vertical cliffs.

Hillsides are prone to landslides after rain. Zigzag upwards or downwards. You could try using trees to slow your descent, but beware touching vines or shrubs with spines or stinging hairs.

River crossings

STREAMS AND RIVERS criss-cross the jungle, forming a barrier to onward travel. A day's hike may involve many crossings. Always take care when crossing water, remember some of **the jungle's deadliest animals may lurk here**.

Where to cross

Walk along the river to find the best crossing point. Good points to cross are where the water is shallow, especially with small rocks. Gravel beds or sandbanks are also safer crossing points, and if you can use large rocks as stepping stones, even better.

← Try to help other group members when crossing water. Remember rocks can be slippery.

Where not to cross

Avoid bends on a river, where the current flows swiftly on the outside. Stay away from steep, slippery banks or white water, and avoid areas just above a waterfall. You could be swept over.

CROSSING SAFELY

1. Undo the belt of your rucksack, so you can discard it if you fall.
2. Use your staff to check the water depth then use it for support while crossing.
3. Keep your boots on.
4. Aim diagonally downriver. Don't fight the current by aiming straight across.
5. Keep watch upstream for debris being swept downriver.
6. Check yourself for leeches as soon as you leave the water.

← Follow the river until you find a stretch that looks crossable. There may be a makeshift bridge. If in doubt, do not cross.

Place the lightest person in the middle when crossing in a line.

Crossing in a group

Crossing with others is a lot safer than going it alone. You can link arms and cross in a line, parallel to the water flow. Or form a huddle like a rugby scrum, with three people facing inwards. Don't forget to keep an eye upstream.

TIP

Don't enter water in the Amazon with an open wound. The smell of blood may attract a feeding frenzy of piranhas.

➡ When huddling as a group, the strongest person should face upstream.

MAKE YOUR GEAR INTO A FLOAT

Use tarpaulin, a plastic poncho or a flysheet to protect your gear if you have to swim for it.

1. Place rucksack and other gear in the middle of the sheet. Add any empty plastic cans and bottles, which will add buoyancy.
2. Fold the sides over and secure tightly with rope or string. If you have a second sheet or bivvy bag, wrap it around the first. Tie the ends tightly.
3. Enter the water and tow your gear behind you.

➡ Use a strap to keep a tight grip on your gear when crossing fast-flowing water.

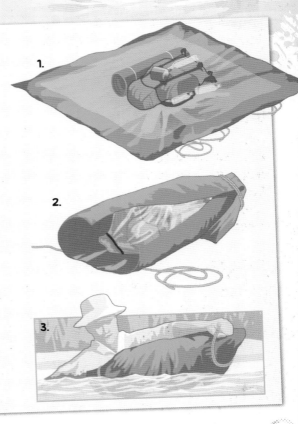

1.

2.

3.

River journeys

RAINFOREST PEOPLES use rivers as highways. Early European explorers used them to penetrate dense jungles. Rivers still offer a quick and easy mode of jungle travel, but **beware water hazards**.

BUILD A BAMBOO RAFT

Bamboo is light but strong. Bamboo poles have airtight sections that make them great for raft-building.

1 Use a machete to cut thick bamboo poles about 3 m long. Beware splinters. Use a knife to make holes right through the poles at both ends and in the centre.

2 Thread slim canes, green sticks or rope through the holes and tie the ends tightly. If you can't make holes, use slimmer poles as cross struts to lash the raft together.

3 Make a second layer of poles and lash it on top.

➡ Notching the ends of the poles will prevent the ropes from slipping.

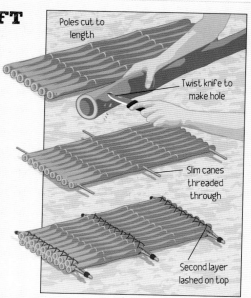

Poles cut to length

Twist knife to make hole

Slim canes threaded through

Second layer lashed on top

⬅ These trekkers are using long poles to raft along a fairly shallow, slow-moving river.

Launching and disembarking

Tie all your gear onto the raft before launching. Tie yourself on too, except when rafting in wild water. Get on and off one at a time. Pull the raft up the bank if possible, or tie securely to a tree. Heavy rain could make the river rise. You don't want to see your raft drifting downstream!

MAKE A PADDLE TO STEER YOUR RAFT

Make a paddle by lashing together several lengths of bamboo to make a flat surface.

Bamboo is split then tied tightly

Shorter piece of bamboo inserted into split

Add more lengths of bamboo

1 Split the top of a bamboo pole, then tie the base of the split. Insert a shorter length of bamboo. Use a square lashing to keep it in place.

2 Add more lengths of bamboo and lash them together. Once your paddle is long enough, tie the end tightly.

River hazards

Perils can come thick and fast on a river. Watch for overhanging branches that could sweep you off the raft, and beware strong currents and tides near the river mouth. Keep watch for rapids and waterfalls ahead. Misty spray can signal a waterfall. You may also hear a roaring sound, or feel the current speeding up. Head for shore immediately. Tie up and investigate on foot.

➡ Keep a sharp eye downsteam for rapids and waterfalls, which could spell disaster.

➡ A Peruvian girl paddles a dugout down a swollen waterway.

Forest canoe

Rainforest peoples make dugout canoes from single treetrunks. Thin sides and a thick base make these craft more stable. The biggest canoes, hewn from large trunks, hold 20 people or more.

TIP

If rapids or a waterfall lie ahead, disembark and carry your gear along the bank until you reach calm water. Send one person back to release the raft. Wade in to recover it if the water is very calm.

75

JUNGLE AIRCRASH
Juliane Koepcke

In 1971, German teenager Juliane Koepcke was on a flight to meet her father. The plane was struck by lightning and exploded, plummeting Juliane into the Peruvian jungle.

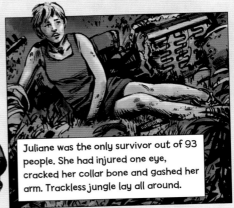

Juliane was the only survivor out of 93 people. She had injured one eye, cracked her collar bone and gashed her arm. Trackless jungle lay all around.

Juliane remembered her father's advice: Heading downriver will lead to civilization. She followed a river for days, wading in the water. She heard helicopters, but had no way to signal for help.

On day 10 Juliane stumbled across a shelter and a moored boat. No one was there but she found petrol and salt, which she used to remove worms that had burrowed into her skin.

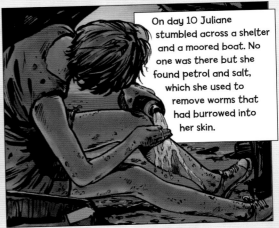

The next day, two men returned to the shelter to find a teenage girl in a miniskirt, covered with scratches. They took her by canoe to the nearest town, where she was taken to hospital.

Juliane was reunited with her father, and they returned to Germany after she made a full recovery. In 2011 she published a book about her ordeal.

GET OUT

Health and emergency

Staying healthy

STAYING IN TOP FORM is vital in the cut-throat world of the jungle. Learning basic first aid could save a life in an emergency. Attending to simple hygiene will help you stay fit and keep you **feeling positive**.

SUNBLOCK
Rays are deflected from the skin's surface

SUNSCREEN
Some rays still penetrate the skin

Protect your skin

The sun is fierce in the tropics. Sunburn can do lasting damage and lead to skin cancer. Apply sun block or high-factor sunscreen to exposed skin and under thin clothes. Reapply if you get wet. Calamine lotion or a damp cloth can help to soothe sunburnt skin.

← Sunblock provides a barrier against the sun's rays, preventing skin damage. Sunscreen allows some rays to penetrate, but still protects your skin.

Health and hygiene

Infections take hold incredibly quickly in hot, damp conditions. Washing helps to combat infection, so take every chance you get to wash. Don't forget to brush your teeth.

TIP
To lower the risk of diarrhoea, make sure all food is prepared in clean conditions and is well cooked. Peel all fruit and boil all water.

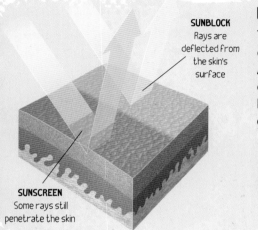

← Wetting your head can lower your body temperature and help to prevent sunstroke.

Jungle illness

ON A JUNGLE TRIP you are mostly likely to be struck down by illnesses related to hot, humid conditions. Jungles are breeding grounds for bugs and bacteria, as well as for all manner of beasts that **itch, bite or sting**.

HEAT-RELATED ILLNESS

Never underestimate the danger of heat. Listen to your body, and if you start to feel ill, take immediate action.

Heat exhaustion

This can strike after strenuous exertion.

Symptoms:
Headache, dizziness, nausea, rapid breathing, sweating.

Treatment:
Lie patient in the shade with head supported. Drink water. Raise legs to improve circulation.

➡ Left untreated, if only for a short time, heat exhaustion can lead to heatstroke. Never ignore symptoms.

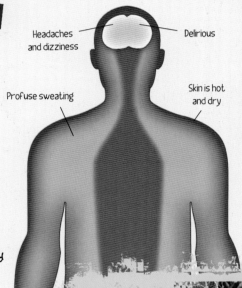

Headaches and dizziness

Delirious

Profuse sweating

Skin is hot and dry

Heatstroke

This occurs when the body's temperature regulation system fails. Potentially fatal.

Symptoms:
Headache, nausea, high temperature, lack of coordination. Patient may become delirious or unconscious. Sweating stops.

Treatment:
Lie patient in the shade with head supported. Remove outer clothes, cool by covering patient in a wet sheet, or by using a wet sponge, until temperature falls.

Trench foot

Infection can set in if your feet are permanently wet. If left untreated, trench foot can lead to gangrene. Always dry your feet thoroughly at the end of each day, and put on dry footwear.

➡ Countless streams in the jungle make it practically impossible to keep feet dry.

WOW!

Juliane Koepcke (see page 76) was tormented by burrowing maggots on her hike to safety. She bent a ring she was wearing into a hook to dig maggots out of her skin.

Stings and bites

Keep calm and allow the insect to remove its sting. If the sting is left in the skin, remove it with tweezers. Be careful not to squeeze the poison sac. With spiders or snakes, lie the person down and wash the wound gently. Prop the patient so that the heart is ABOVE the wound site. Bandage the limb tightly well above the wound. Keep the patient still and seek urgent medical help.

➡ A bee stinging. Swift removal of the stinger will stop more venom entering the body.

⬅ Bixa orellana is a shrub from tropical America. Local people use the leaves to treat heartburn, digestive problems and skin infections. The red seeds are used to flavour food and as a dye.

TIP

Caterpillar or tarantula hairs can be removed with sticky duct tape. Simply place tape over the affected area and pull it off again.

Jungle remedies

Rainforest people use hundreds of natural remedies. Various plants are used to ease pain, relieve swelling, heal infection and get rid of parasites. Medicinal plants are grown near the village, so the right medicine is always to hand.

Keeping safe

KNOWING BASIC FIRST AID will help you deal with minor injuries. If a serious accident strikes, you should seek medical help as soon as possible. In a remote jungle you may have to do what you can, using **whatever materials are to hand**.

Assessing an emergency

Assess the surroundings, if someone in your group has an accident, check for danger before helping them. Don't put your own life at risk. Assess the casualty by checking the person's life signs. Check the casualty for injuries. Do they respond if questioned? If not, pinch one earlobe firmly. If there is no response, he or she may be unconscious.

Recovery position

Put an unconscious but breathing patient into the recovery position to prevent further injury. Roll the casualty on his or her side, with one arm under the head for support. The hand tilts to keep the airways open. Bend one leg to hold the pose.

EMERGENCY PRIORITIES

1. Assess the scene. Protect or remove yourself from danger first. You cannot help others if you are at risk.
2. Call for help and remain calm.
3. Check for breathing and pulse. If the casualty isn't breathing, you will have to carry out chest compressions and rescue breaths.
4. If the casualty is unconscious but breathing, place them in the recovery position (see below).
5. Check for injuries, and staunch bleeding with direct pressure.

Step 2

Step 1

Roll the person onto their side

Place upper leg at a right-angle to the body

Tuck upper hand under chin

Step 3

Tilt head back and lift chin

Bring leg forward for support

⬆ Putting an unconscious person in the recovery position keeps their airway clear and prevents choking.

Preventing infection

Bacteria thrive in jungles. Even small cuts and grazes can quickly become infected. Be sure to clean and sterilize all wounds using antiseptic wipes. Staunch bleeding by pressing a bandage, cloth or even your hand on the wound site. When bleeding stops, cleanse the wound with sterile water or antiseptic. Apply a clean dressing.

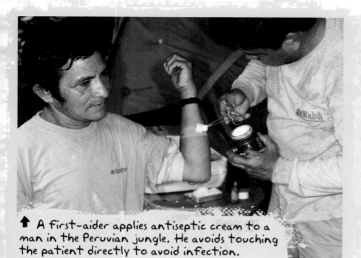

⬆ A first-aider applies antiseptic cream to a man in the Peruvian jungle. He avoids touching the patient directly to avoid infection.

RIVER RESCUE

1 Don't enter the water to save someone else – doing so could put yourself in danger.

2 Lie down on the bank. Use a tree or vine to anchor yourself.

3 Reach out with a long branch. Alternatively, throw a rope. Twist the rope around a tree so you don't get pulled in.

TIP

Make an emergency bandage by tearing a t-shirt into strips, and a belt can be used as a sling. A broken limb can be cushioned with clothing.

Jungle stitches

Rainforest people use army ants to close wounds that need stitches. The ant is held just above the wound. When it bites down, its jaws clamp the wound together. The body is then twisted off, leaving the head. Several ants are used to seal a large cut.

⬆ An army ant clamps its jaws into human skin. The strong jaws are designed to cut up food and prey.

Attracting rescue

IF YOU GET IN SERIOUS TROUBLE, you will need to signal for help. However, the dense cover of the jungle makes it very hard to attract attention. It's best to signal from **a clearing or by a stream**.

FIRE PLATFORM

Fire and smoke signals cannot be seen through dense canopy. Light a fire in a clearing or on a raft moored on water. Make a small raft for the fire using the technique on page 52. Cover the base with earth as on page 29. Tether the raft to the bank. Light as soon as you hear a plane.

↑ Anchor the raft to both banks so it doesn't drift to the edge.

CONTACTING EMERGENCY SERVICES

1. Note nearby landscape features that could be seen from the air, such as cliffs or rivers. Be ready to describe your distance and direction from these features.
2. If there has been an accident, be ready to give details of the number of casualties, injuries and the patients' conditions.

↓ Use a global positioning system (GPS) device to locate your position if you have one. This system works by using signals from three or more satellites to find your exact position.

Using a mobile phone

Keep trying your mobile phone to see if you can get a signal. If you can, contact or text the emergency number of your service provider. Key in the number before you go. If you don't have a signal, try turning your mobile on and off in an SOS pattern. Don't waste the battery by leaving the phone on.

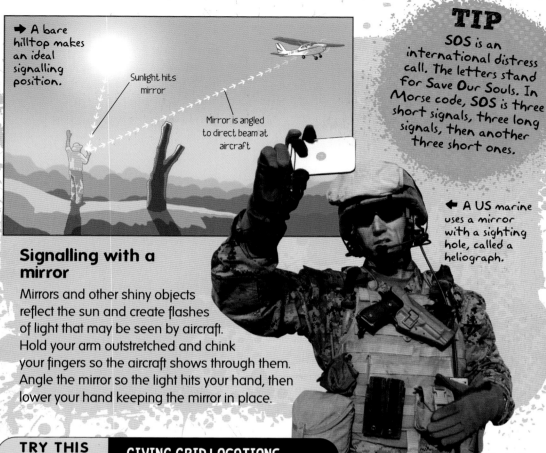

→ A bare hilltop makes an ideal signalling position.

Sunlight hits mirror

Mirror is angled to direct beam at aircraft

TIP

SOS is an international distress call. The letters stand for Save Our Souls. In Morse code, SOS is three short signals, three long signals, then another three short ones.

← A US marine uses a mirror with a sighting hole, called a heliograph.

Signalling with a mirror

Mirrors and other shiny objects reflect the sun and create flashes of light that may be seen by aircraft. Hold your arm outstretched and chink your fingers so the aircraft shows through them. Angle the mirror so the light hits your hand, then lower your hand keeping the mirror in place.

TRY THIS AT HOME — GIVING GRID LOCATIONS

If you raise help on your mobile, give your location by using the map grid reference. Grid numbers are marked in a map's margins. Practise on a local map, by finding the grid reference for your home. You should give the east-west distance first – the letters along the bottom – then the north-south distance – the numbers up the side.

→ Use grid references to to provide information about your whereabouts. Can you spot the river source in A2?

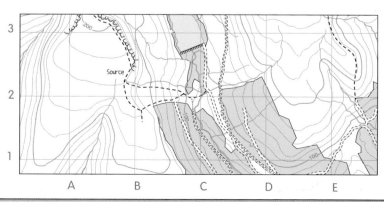

Source

Leaving the jungle

YOUR JUNGLE TRIP IS ENDING, whether you are being rescued or finishing an expedition. The jungle will have taught you many lessons about surviving in the wild, which will be useful on **your next trip**.

Rescue by air

Helicopters can only land in a clearing. If the pilot is unable to land, you will have to be winched to safely. Beware – the winch carries a static electric charge from the aircraft. You must allow the winch to touch ground or water before you grab it, or you will get a shock.

← Very often, helicopters are the best means of getting into dense jungle. They can hover low to look for stranded people.

TIP

When you leave camp, make sure everything is as you found it. Pick up any litter. Make sure your fire is out.

Rescue by land

Remain calm and patient if you know that rescue is on the way. If you see rescuers approaching by land, shout to warn them of potential dangers such as cliffs. Listen to any instructions they give you and carry them out exactly.

→ Heavy rain has made driving conditions treacherous for this rescue land rover. Be sure to let rescuers know of any flooding or swollen rivers.

AUSTRALIAN ORDEAL
William Bliss

In 2007, Scottish teenager William Bliss went for a hike in the Australian rainforest. He planned to hike less than 4 km, so he took no food or water.

But William lost the track and started walking in circles. Night fell and the temperature dropped. He was only wearing light clothes, so was bitterly cold.

William had watched many TV survival programmes. He kept warm by making a bed of bracken.

The next day he heard helicopters circling, but the pilots couldn't spot him because of the dense forest canopy.

William was so hungry that he ate watercress from a stream. He found a path but it led nowhere. He spent a second night in the wild.

After he had failed to return, William's girlfriend had alerted the emergency services. On day 3 they found him and whisked him to safety. A little knowledge had helped him survive and emerge from the jungle unharmed.

NOTES

GLOSSARY

Ailment An illness.

Allergic Having an unpleasant reaction to something, such as itching or a rash.

Antiseptic A medicine used to fight infection.

Bushcraft Survival skills such as hunting, navigating and making things that are useful in the wild.

Canopy A dense layer of leaves formed by interlocking branches in a jungle.

Carbohydrate Sugars and starches that provide energy.

Casualty Someone who is injured.

Cloud forest Misty, cloud-swathed forest found on mountain slopes in the tropics.

Contour lines The lines on a map that join places at the same height above sea level.

Cordage Cord, rope or string used for tying.

Constrictor A snake that kills its prey by squeezing it to death.

Flash flood When a river rises very quickly after heavy rain.

Grid reference A method of pinpointing location using the numbered grid of a map.

Heliograph A mirror that is used to reflect sunlight to send signals.

Improvise To make something from materials that are to hand.

Kindling Dry twigs that burn well, used to get a fire going.

Lashings Bindings made of materials such as rope.

Malaria A tropical disease carried by mosquitoes. Malaria can kill.

Nausea A feeling of sickness.

Primary forest Untouched rainforest with ancient trees.

Primates The group of mammals that includes apes and monkeys.

Protein Nutrients found in foods such as meat, fish and eggs, which are vital for health.

Secondary forest Forest that has grown back after being cleared.

Tinder Dry material such as grass, that is used to light fires.

Toxin Poison.

Tributary A minor river or stream that joins a main river.

Tropics The areas on either side of the Equator, where the sun's heat is fierce.

ACKNOWLEDGEMENTS

The publishers would like to thank the following sources for the use of their photographs:
t = top, b = bottom, l = left, r = right, c = centre, bg = background

Front cover (main) Patrick K. Campbell/Shutterstock; (tr) f9photos/Shutterstock.com
Back cover Olga Popova/Shutterstock.com
Alamy 85(t) Morley Read; 87(t) Roger Arnold; 88(b) David Gee 3
Corbis 9(br) Ian Nichols/National Geographic Society; 31(t) Peter McBride/Aurora Photos; 37(b) Chris Linder/Visuals Unlimited; 48(b) Cyril Ruoso/JH Editorial/Minden Pictures; 83(t) Lynda Richardson
FLPA 11(tr) ImageBroker; 18(b) Malcolm Schuyl
Fotolia.com 8 Impala
Getty Images 11(t) Cyril Ruoso/ JH Editorial; 83(b) Michael Langford; 85(b) Visuals Unlimited, Inc./Alex Wild
Glow Images 74(b) Eye Ubiquitous
National Geographic Stock 11(cl) Pete McBride; 29(t) Pete McBride; 37(b) Pete McBride; 39(b) Otis Imboden; 44(t) Tim Laman, (b) Tim Laman; 54(l) Otis Imboden; 57(t) Ed George; 59(b) Bill Hatcher; 65(t) Gordon Wiltsie; 69(t) Pete McBride; 70(t) Stephen Alvarez; 71(bl) Bill Hatcher; 81(b) Pete McBride; 82(b) Pete McBride; 86(b) Stephen Alvarez
NHPA 11(tl) Andrea Bonetti; 12(c) Andre Baertschi; 19(tl) Andrea & Antonella Ferrari, (tr) Stephen Dalton
Photoshot 9(tl) David Slater; 11(bl) Imagebroker.net; 14(t) David Slater; 15(b) Noah Friedman-Rudovsky/WPN; 19(br) Daniel Heuclin; 55(b) Photo Researchers; 71(br) pbnj productions; 75(b) Nigel Smith; 88(t) Noah Friedman-Rudovsky/WPN

Rex Features 13(t) James Morgan/Robert Harding
Shutterstock.com 7 Ralph Loesche; 11(cr) Niar; 12(cl) Photofish; 13(b) Harald Toepfer; 16(tl) Mike Price, (tc) worldswildlifewonders, (tr) neijia, (b) Karen Givens; 17(t) szefei; (b) Pasi Koskela; 18(t) Eric Isselée; 19(bl) ecoventurestravel; 20(t) AJancso, 20(b) Dr. Morley Read; 23 Anton Gvozdikov; 24 Janne Hamalainen; 25(t) Anton Gvozdikov; 26 (from tl to br) E.G.Pors, Alex Staroseltsev, iQoncept, HomeStudio, Lusoimages, k_sasiwimo, Ruslan Semichev, Peter zijlstra, www.rescue-flares.co.uk, Karl Yamashita, Ragnarock, Jason Swalwell, Michael Bann, design56, HomeStudio, Smit, J and S Photography, Maxim Godkin, Coprid, nui7711, Ingridsl, terekhov igor; 27(tl) Dimedrol68, (tr) Gavran333, (cr) Olga Popova, (b) Pedro Salaverría; 28(tl) Teamdaddy, (c) Péter Gudella, (cl) Karkas, (cr) Sean MacD, (b) Gertan; 29(b) IgorXIII; 30(t) Elena Schweitzer, (b) Warren Goldswain; 31(b) Lusoimages; 35 Andrushchenko Dmytro; 36 Robert Adrian Hillman; 38(t) Sebastian Kaulitzki; 42(tl) Diana Taliun, (tc) andersphoto, (tl) vilax, (c) Ruslan Semichev; 43(b) olmarmar; 49 PaintedLens; 50 Frontpage; 53(b) Ildi Papp; 54(tc) crystalfoto, (tr) satit_srihin, (c) Seroff, (br) Tungphoto; 56 Jens Stolt; 57(b) Ilya D. Gridnev; 63 Paul Clarke; 64 Ernita; 67(b) Ben Heys; 68(t) Anton Gvozdikov; 69(b) DJTaylor; 70(b) St. Nick; 71(t) Ralph Loesche; 72(t) Creatista, (b) Libor Píka; 75(c) A.S. Zain; 79 Dr. Morley Read; 80 Brandon Alms; 82 Matthew Cole; 84 hkannn

The publishers would like to thank the following artists who have contributed to this book:
Julian Baker, Stuart Jackson-Carter, Nick Spender

All other images from the Miles Kelly Artwork Bank

Every effort has been made to acknowledge the source and copyright holder of each picture.
Miles Kelly Publishing apologises for any unintentional errors or omissions.